Poppy's Pet Adventure

Written by Krystal Grant

with the help of Madison, Collin and Chase Grant

ILLUSTRATED BY DARIN LORENZO HAGOOD

NOVELS BY KRYSTAL GRANT

Under the Palmetto Tree: A Novella

The Miseducation of Ms. G

Brooklyn

CHILDREN'S BOOKS BY KRYSTAL GRANT

Poppy and the Playdate

Poppy's Pet Adventure

Poppy's Pet Adventure

Krystal Grant

FIRST EDITION

ISBN: 9781948018159

Library of Congress Control Number: 2018900860

Published by Kenely Books, An Imprint of Wyatt-MacKenzie

kenely@wyattmackenzie.com

For little readers everywhere

~Krystal

This book is dedicated to my family

Kayela and William Hagood, Ann and John Hagood,

and those friends who always support my art,

Tina S. and Correy T.

~Darin

Poppy watched Blake play with his dog.

Poppy decided she wanted a pet.

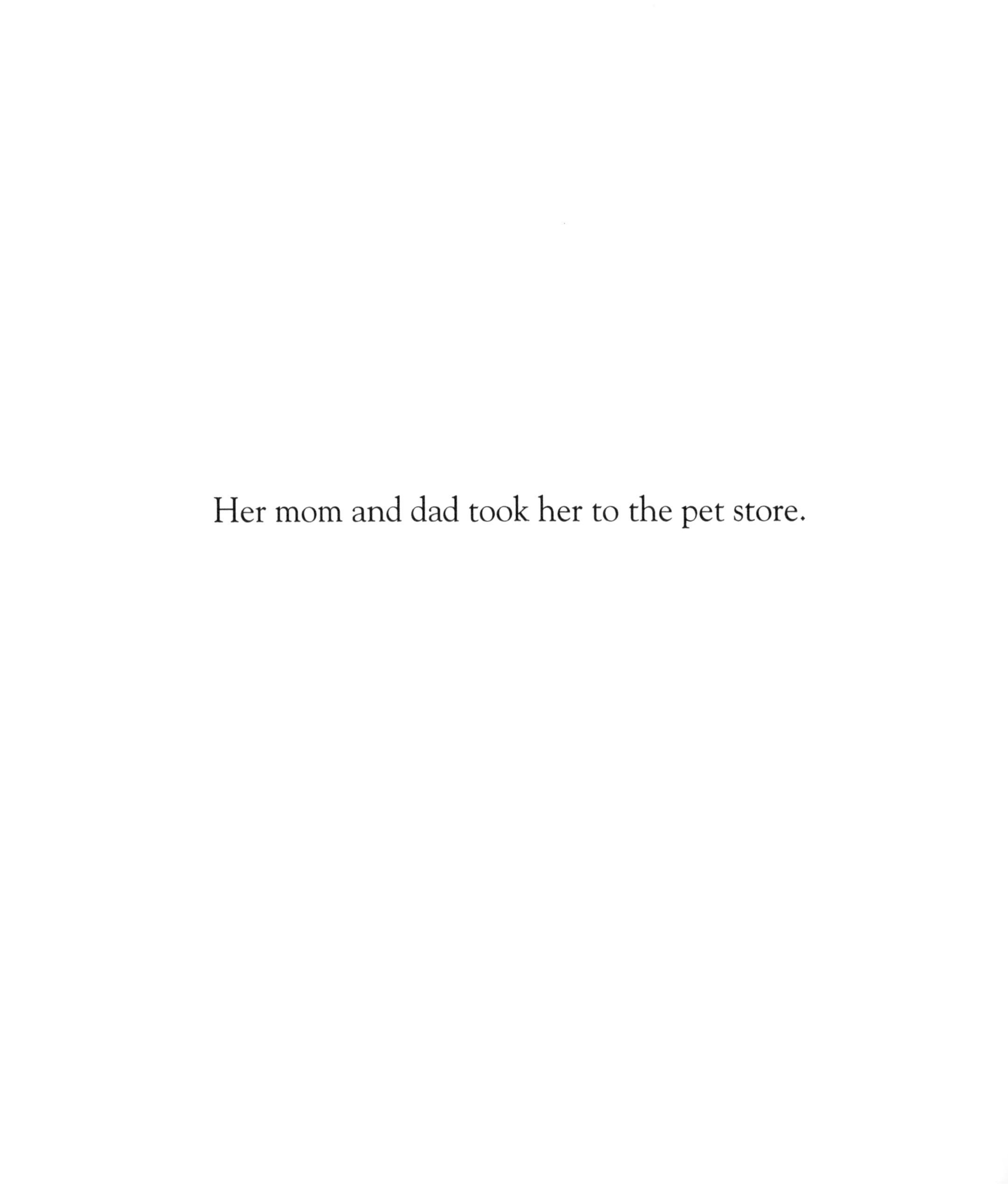

Her mom and dad took her to the pet store.

PETSTORE

Poppy saw birds and hamsters.

She saw lizards and fish.

FISH
Reptiles

Poppy even saw a snake.

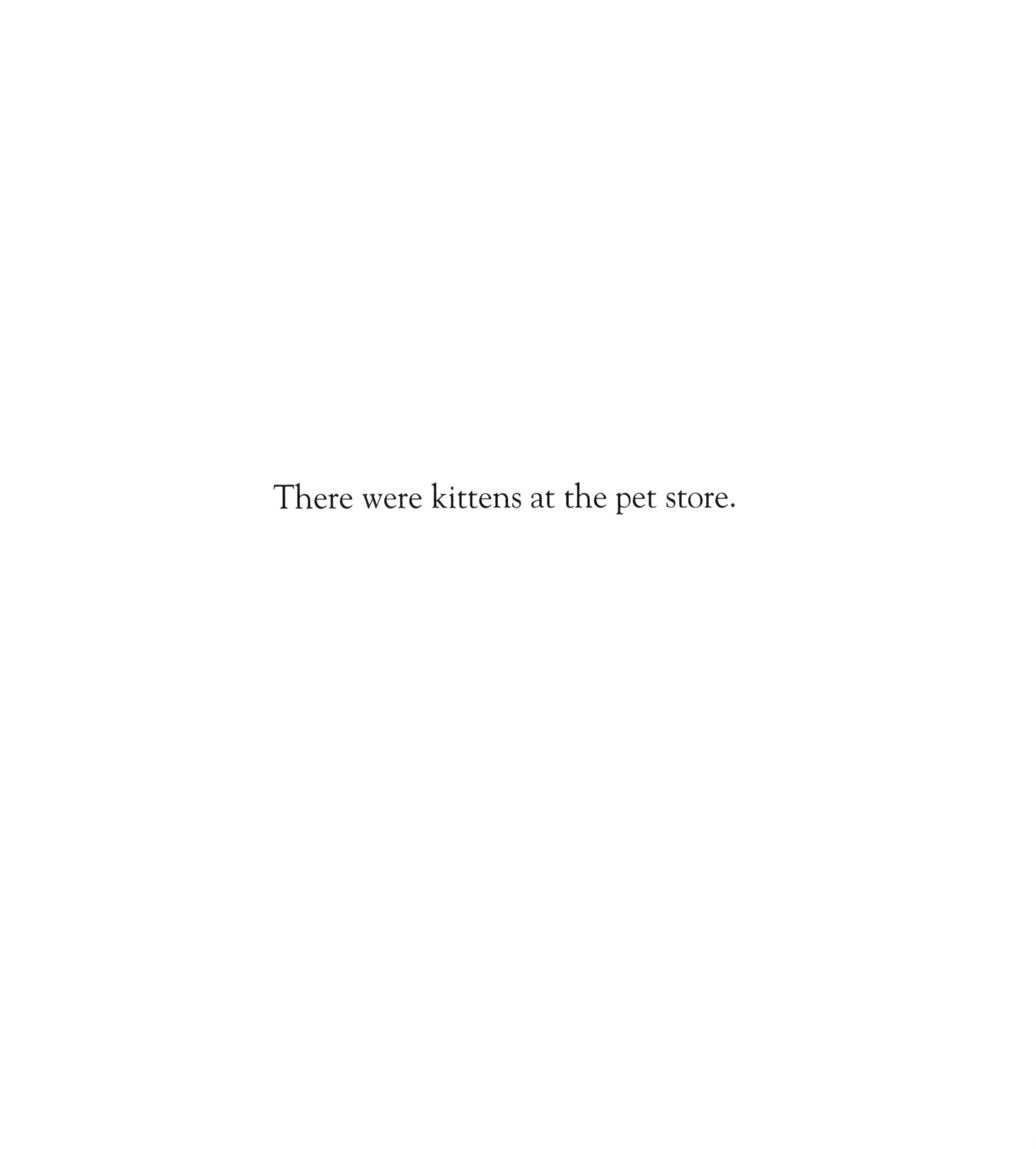

There were kittens at the pet store.

And a few rabbits.

Poppy couldn't decide what kind of pet she wanted.

She walked all around the store.

Poppy saw a little brown puppy in a cage.

The puppy looked at Poppy and wagged its tail.

Poppy smiled.

She asked her dad if the little brown puppy could be her pet.

Her dad said, “YES”!

Poppy took the puppy home.

She gave him food and water.

She even gave him a bath!

Poppy played with her puppy every day.

He was the perfect pet.

The End

Author's Note

For three years I had the esteemed pleasure of working as a kindergarten teacher. It was a far cry from my many years teaching high school literature. Each day, my four and five year olds walked through my classroom door with bright eyes filled with wonder and excitement.

Our favorite part of the day was circle time. We would all sit criss cross apple sauce on my colorful carpet and immerse ourselves in stories told by amazing authors. Often times, I'd lose my voice because I read the stories with such volume and vigor. The students buckled over in laughter at my antics.

Being an educator is one of my greatest joys. I hope this book serves as a beacon of joy for your little one. Happy reading, my friends.

www.ingramcontent.com/pod-product-compliance
Lightning Source LLC
LaVergne TN
LVHW060643110826
845147LV00018B/1034